Praise for David

OUT COMES BUTCH:
"...a gifted actor and wickedly funny writer."
– Laurence Bommer, *Chicago Reader*

"Half the audience wanted his blood, the other half would have happily settled for his autograph."
– Felix Green - *The Voice, Britain's Best Black Newspaper*

"With breathtaking cheek and speed it charts one man's hysterical circular odyssey through every sexual stereotype imaginable."
–Joyce McMillan, *The Guardian*

TOKENS: A PLAY ON THE PLAGUE:
"Brilliant, powerful theater. I am all admiration for the wonders of the show."
– Nancy Scott, *San Francisco Examiner*

"Anyone interested in theater should see it. It is magnificent."
– A.J. Esta, *Hollywood Dramalogue*

"TOKENS became a kind of stripping back to the essence of theater, a creation of art from the panorama of human experience."
– Alan Rich, *California Magazine.*

BORDER-X-FRONTERA (written with Guillermo Gomez Peña):
"Border-X-Frontera is an intensely personal political work, a paragon of what performance art radio can be at it's best."
– Jacki Apple, *LA Reader*

REVERENCE FOR THE DEAD (Ozball the Musical):
"Schein's take on the media culture and its obsession with violence is wickedly funny and keenly observed, and his writing is sharp thorugh the piece. The songs that Schein and J. Raoul Brody have created together are terrific."
– Elliott Smith, *The Daily Californinan*

LIFE IS NOT A COUNTRY WESTERN SONG:
"This is remarkable playwriting delivered with remarkable cadences and dexterity."
– Marti Keller, *Berkely Gazette*

MYethiOPIA:
"Both funny and heart-wrenching, the show is a non-stop rollercoaster of personal and public calamities and victories, all delivered with great skill, energy and honesty."
– Judith Marcuse, Director, International Centre for Art and Social Change

THE BOG PEOPLE:. "...gathered force as it thundered along. A ritual of human sacrifice enacted in spare, dark terms an with a made-up language inveneted by David Schein, its small knot of peformers convincingly suggested the fury of a possessed mob."
– Misha Berson, *Bay Guardian*

DIE RUCKKEHR DER JUDIN: (The Return of the Jewish Woman - written with Pit Hartmann and Barara Kemmler):
"Astonishingly relevant. A fight for remembrance is on our heels."
– Werner Hiese, *IVZ Münster*

Other Works by David Schein

Out Comes Butch - West Coast Plays 17/18
Publisher: California Theatre Council (1985)
ASIN: B003O1VFZQ

"Incident in Awassa" - *The American Theatre Reader: Essays
and Conversations from American Theatre Magazine*
Staff of American Theatre Magazine (Editor)
ISBN 978-1-55936-346-2

My Murder and Other Local News

David Schein

Fomite
Burlington, Vt

ISBN-13: 978-1-937677-74-9
Library of Congress Control Number: 2014945828

Fomite
58 Peru Street
Burlington, VT 05401
www.fomitepress.com

Cover image — Tod Thilleman
Author photo — Susan Schein

To C.P.

Let's do more
+ more

Much love

Oakland 10/21/15

Author's Note

Dear Reader: these are *performance poems* which chronicle dramatic events in the middle age of my life in Chicago between 1994 and the year 2000. I've presented them in theaters in Vermont, Chicago, California and Europe. Imagine them *acted* as well as on the page.

To the women of my life, Dana, Aurora, Sue and Flo.

Contents

My Murder

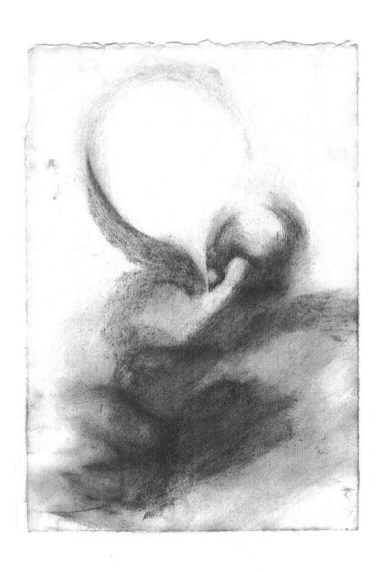

My Murder

I.

If I could pin
the face of the boy who raised that bat
and brought it down so wordlessly on the head of the other boy
to one of the hundreds of Polaroids the cops showed me
that night
the case might break and they might get their man
which is too large a word for this kid.

He stood in front of me
long enough for anyone to snap
ten shots
before he crossed the street with his partner
snuck up on that boy at the bus stop
raised a bat and broke his skull open.

The cops have been here twice with their photographs
asking me of what I'm absolutely sure.

That his head was shaved
that he was fourteen fifteen
had a fox face
and looked more Puerto Rican than Mexican
that he and another boy popped out
from behind a red truck
and were suddenly on the sidewalk
not five feet in front of me
talking code with head jerks like a couple at a party
as I sipped my Margarita on the restaurant patio
and watched the conversation of their eyes
imagining stupidly something like:
"You wanna eat here?" "Fuck no lets go"
in hindsight dead wrong and blind
to where they would not look
the bus-stop across the street behind them
where their target waited with his girl.

II.

My daughter likes the leather and gun-oil smell
of the big cops with their summer shorts
shoulder holsters and sizzling radios.
She grabs at the pictures on the living room floor
scattering my piles of Possibles Not Likelies
and Definitely Nots
thinking them toys brought by the big men
for Daddy and her to play with
like her cards
of colorful clowns and clouds
but no
these boys slouch in the Thirteenth Tac Squad's flash:
black boys tan boys light boys
piles of faces.

Definitely Nots
too black too white too old
Not Likelies
too fat too square too round
Possibles
young light-skinned
fawn faced like Felix the son of Maria
the woman who cares for my daughter.
Felix with a teardrop tattoo from prison left beneath his eye
so remarkably tender with my two year old
has been in jail for two months
and is not a candidate
but his face takes over my memory
as my girl kicks the pictures I've so carefully sorted
into one big heap on the floor.

"Did you hear them say anything?" "No
they were silent"
but the way they turned
screamed
a turn in three parts
so strange.
First part
leading with the head "There he is"
"OK"
and turning back
then a half-step with shoulder elbow hip
cocked
"Are you ready?"
"Yeah"
then turning back then "Here we go"
and so they turned
and walked out of my field of interest.

They've decided not to dine
I thought
getting back to my drink
hopeful
that my wife would prolong her walk
with our baby girl who so loves to fish for ice
it's hard to drink in peace
when that swing
smashed
the corner of my eye wide open
to see that bat come down on that boy
and another swing that brought him to the pavement.
The woman screaming "Stop it stop it stahhhhp it"
finally clicked the shutter in my brain to tell me
this is <u>not</u> a picture, this is happening
finally set me running
inside
to call for help.

But in that replay I cross the street, chair in hand
to block the second swing
and use the kick from the dojo
"Crane-claw with Twist"
to send the bat flying
and in that replay I calmly shoot
one of bad-boys in the ass from my chair
with the gun Dad gave me
for my bar miztvah
and in that replay I tackle the boy with the bat
and the boy who got beat gets up bloody
shoots me
and runs.

7

III.
Two years ago The Lovers on this side of Western
left
pushed by The Lords to California and Fullerton.
The Lords are related to The Kings and The Kings rule.
This is the gospel according to Dennis
my neighbor
who has lived here through waves of Hillbillies
Puerto Ricans and Mexicans. He says it's getting better.
Theresa at the Park whose brother is a Joker
has another theory.
Some Cobras told her that the kid with the bat
was a Disciple and the guy he hit
was a Lover
who had "done something"
so he showed heart by wacking him back.

Two doctors who'd been dining called the shots.
"DON'T move him. WAIT! They'll be here
in a MINUTE! WAIT!"
keeping the girl off him.
She tried to hold him
keep him awake keep his eyes open
and they held her back to stop her from shaking him
as she pleaded
"Stay strong Manuel, hang in there Manuel.
Don't die. Stay strong."
Manuel shuddering howling in pain,
fought to stay in the world
as his heels clattered on the pavement
and when the cops arrived they asked me
"Now what exactly did you see?"

The same face I saw
behind the fist in my face on a riverbank
in Iowa
in the flickering globe of world neighborhood news
respewed
to harden in the mind's eye;
the cop puts his pistol to the temple of the VC suspect
in the famous newsreel
POP and he falls down.
The smiling Serb poses for TIME
with his boot on the face of a body
in Vukovar.
It was a lovely summer night.
when I could not put the same old story
in a box
and no one could render with make-up
the dent and the dead eye floating like an egg in red
and I could not click the girl sobbing "how could they do that?
how could they do that?" off
and I could not adjust the tympany of heels
to any sense.

I could not imagine what I'd seen.

IV.
The blonde cop says they wacked the wrong dude
some guy too old to be still
gang-banging. How old? "He won't see twenty
not if his brain swells."
Part of his head was dented in
soft red wet above the temple
a sunken patch.
I saw that much before the cops came
after I ran with the pack of men from the restaurant
to the screaming woman and the boy on the concrete
to find the punks
gone.

Johnnie Bolero ran with me and his face twisted
when he saw the boy's eye
sobbed "Oh my god"
and covered his face with his hands as if he'd been hit
but later said if the cops kept coming into his restaurant
bothering him at "peak" about the "incident"
with their pictures and their questions
he'd "punch 'em out."
"They scare the customers.
Business was booming
until this."

V.

Piles of faces. Pieces
of features.
The cops say that some I've picked are dead
and others are in prison.
"There's a lot of scum out there.
We're just scratching the surface."
They say they'll be back
and if something else comes to me I should not hesitate
to call.
They take their pictures. My daughter cries.
She wants to see more boys.
She wants the men to share their toys.

I don't. Next day
Restaurant Johnny tells me "some kids" came in and asked
about the man
who told the cops he'd seen the beating
so I call
with this detail
the cops
ask them to keep a lower profile
not to come to the front door
to meet me in a restaurant
or at the station.
That night a squad car squawks by my stoop
and three cops clump noisily up my stairs to tell me
not to worry
then leave boisteriously bantering on the street
about the Cubs.

I shave my beard
cut my hair
on walks with my daughter
watch my back and cars.
I think I see him in a pick-up truck
memorize the plate
phone it in.
The skinny shaved-headed boys
with bats in their eyes
are everywhere.

VI.

Two weeks later Manuel dies.
The cops say the kid "did us all a service"
because Manuel
was a real bad guy
with notches on his own bat
had done time for manslaughter
taken life before his was batted away.
The letter from the victim-witness division of the State's
Attorney's office
says PEOPLE vs. Donald Gonzalez
CHARGE: Murder
CASE NO. 96CR -21681
JUDGE: Mary Maxwell Thomas.
I may be called to witness
and if any problems have arisen as a result of the crime
The victim-witness coordinator would like to assist me in any
possible way.

Dear victim witness coordinator:
Please tell me how to end this poem.

VII.

In this ending
Donald Gonzales
when viewed through the one-way mirror
looks like more like that killer kid might look
with hair
than the other boys in the line-up
though his ears are wrong.

After I make him the cops say that Manuel's girl has picked him
too.
At sunset
the shadow of a doubt can dwarf whatever casts it
but in the high noon of indignation I can split the difference
between what I saw and what I remember.

Case closed.
At the trial I beg leeway
for bad eyes and poor memory
not "absolutely sure" but "90% positive."
The jury buys a confession clearly extracted with batons.
Gonzales takes the time he was born to get without expression
and swims in the water of prison with jail-bird gills.
Paroled in fifteen years
he's popped in a month for something else
he didn't do.
He can't seem to get off
or be stabbed in the jail wars deep enough to die.
As a ripe old con he robs a bank
just to get back in
but pulls it off.

By that time the secret of his ears is buried
with me.

Or this ending:
I am prosecuted for astigmatism
and painted
as a fool in the news.
"No my glasses were not on." "Yes I need them."
Confession thrown out
the kid walks.
At night the Lovers' super woofers pulse by my house.
Bone-tired
I wake too late to smoke and crackling flame.
The papers love the story of the double death
mother and baby of witness
fire bombed.
The cops haul in every Lover and their mother.
I want to leave the planet
but am trapped
in a skin graft
funerals
unending trials and fury.
In Alaska later I marry again.
My "new life" grows slowly like bones
under leather.

Or this:
The kid gets Death.
The new law says
the family can watch.

Is this better?
Gonzales has an alibi
gets off.
They never find who did it.
Nothing more of this murder
compounds its own sadness.

VIII.

I ask the kids I work with
Tameka and Happi
where to put these little killers:
Tameka sent her daddy up
when he stole her pay for crack
Happi's brother's out again
hanging in the house while Moms works.
A nanny named Trauma taught these kids to dance.
They know too well the dead boys
murder boys wounded boys
and say
"Jail don't fix shit
it just concentrates it.
They should mother him
smother him in expensive programmatic love
but if that don't work
ice him.
Fourteen? Too old. He's lost. Too late. He's gone.
Get him off the street.
You've got to reach them when they're five"
though Happi recalls a ten year old who killed somebody
"his father maybe"
who's now in college.

IX.

Yet no resolution
line-up or summons jangles this splinter
from my brain.
Someone in Juvie waits for trial
and I wait for the larger indictment
as if it will ever come
as if this tiny chip of terror
will ever fit any pattern of best intentions
of goodness justice
tip the balance
so that
a million refugees in the hills of Goma
will find water from a rock
and all that happens
will have reason.

THE FLOOD OF '93

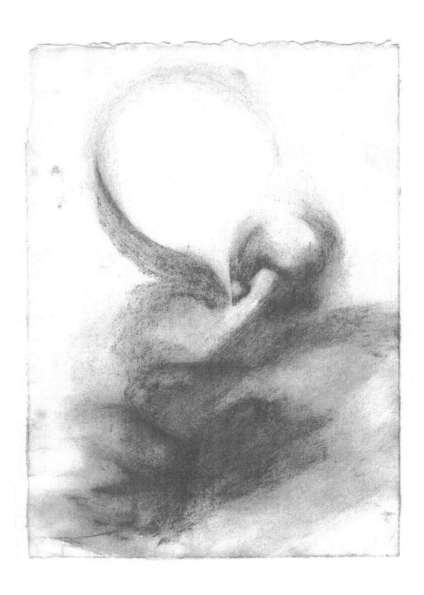

THE FLOOD OF '93

See down
red mud
through furrows of clouds.
I fly over
the flood
to my Dad's
open heart.

It's a mess.
Ol' Miss is
over its banks.
Treetops snake parallel
to archipelagos of roofs
fields rise
out of lakes and curve
back under.
The river's hemorrhaging.
Imagine scuba farmers
harvesting bottom corn.
Look for bubbles.
Tie a stone
around lunch.

They've shaved his chest
sawed through
the breast
dammed the incalculable
torrents of blood
opened to the light
the gristly pipes of
the big motor
that runs him.

Put in the main line.
Drive the tubes
through the innards.
All the kings men
try to put the red
back in the egg
sandbags
and ditches reamed
quick in the dirt. Still
the levee holds.

Pine stubble.
Mountain face.
Forks of the river
join the trunk.
The lines from the legs
meet the middle.
Beyond where the capillaries
lazy line-doodle
through the unfenced fatlands
the vast cellular outback

smells of Brooklyn
school yard
onions
laboratory chemicals
love-sweat and baby shit
sharper than in waking life.
From the sky
the shadow
dwarfs its cloud.

See ahead
his Arizona
paper bag skin
dry flowers on
the boneless chin.
This is what we all grind down to
blade carved mesa
miles between breath
between water.

I'm over irrigated
desert
now Phoenix
as they cinch the valves
tight into the coronary vessels
gut-stitch the heart's lips shut
and Dad endures
his body—his scar.
Can life survive
this prolonging?

He has six tubes coming out of him now.

Arnold
father
replicator
my liquid
fossil
sperm shooter.
This dun colored crust
must be your Nevada.
That dammed blue lake
squirts juice through wires
to Las Vegas.

Lights and Beepers.
Lights and Beepers.
He's on two pumps and a pace maker
as they jump-start
jump start
jump start
the heart.
Too traumatized to
turn over
it doesn't respond
to shock. Later
the partial autopsy
says why says why says
why.

Death Valley
gone in a minute.
Now the Sierra
still white in July
with this year's huge snow
Yosemite
Falls
picks up the sun down there.
He's closed up
out of the OR and into the ICU.
Angels in face-masks
hair bags rubber gloves
man the pumps
deliver timed electric jolts
work on him   in him   for him
but still the damned
oxygen starved
clogged old rot-bag
won't kick.

I'm over the aorta
of California
the hydrologically engineered
Valley of Lushness
when they take him off
the machine.
He stops living.
He resumes.
I land.
The coast range
dreams
in its fog.

My mother reads the gauges
shakes her head.
Flo knows.
It's not the first time
she's almost lost this heart.
A triple bypass eight
angioplasties all
covered bought nine
more years.
She returns
eyes full
to the waiting room
reads
eyes full
her Romance.

It stops again.
They get it going.

I transport South
in a white van cell
down a clogged freeway
to the hospital
follow Flo's beacon
straight to the waiting
room. "Not good
we nearly lost him.
Go in and see.
he's painted purple
iodine from the chest up.
They're working on him."

Last shot.
Looking at his watch
at the airport
in a hurry. Is there time?
We'd hiked the Indian Burial Mounds
above the Mother of the waters
a month before the flood
hit Marquette
with a ton of muck
him smiling hard
as he popped his Nitro.
He didn't look forward
to sorting out his heart
again
his "See ya" meant "Don't bet on it."
I didn't want to
see him
tubed up purple out cold
in the ICU

if this was it.

He fights his vegetable fight
dreams old tree dreams
as his pulse recedes
decades fly backwards
he loves my mother
a thousand times again
and others he never got to

27

pees on his brother for revenge
extracts from his own blood
the chemical formula
for kindness
his synthesis wins prizes
it's oral application
makes millions.

She shakes her head.

"Respitory Therapist to ICU.
Respitory Therapist to ICU."
Her eyes leave
her book.
His last gasp?
She holds herself
down in the chair
wants to
doesn't
has to
can't
watch him
give it up.
He'd taken his bow
before he'd gone under
laughed his epitaph
to the gurney pushers.
"Where are your pitchforks?
Why aren't you wearing black?"

Whumpf
the bright wave crashes
rocks him.
Fizzzzzzz
the undertow sucks him back in.
The doctors crowd us
either side
Nurse and Surgeon
cut us like herd dogs
away from the other cardiac
families in the waiting room.
"We did everything we could."
The surgeon
surprised at the heart's failure
explains the technical
ramifications of Arnold's death.
His scientific talk
animates my scientist
mother. She understands.
the condition of the arteries.
I wonder if they blew it.

I call my sister.
She will fly tomorrow.
I call the three brothers
to say the second is
the first
fast before they
get a chance to ask anything.
"I've got bad news.

Dad died an hour ago"
        and wait
        as the flood
of images of images of images
        clobbers them

                the kid
                brother
                youth
                        young man
                        father
                        grandpa
                old man
                dead man
                beat them to it.

        About the arrangements
        they will change next week's plans
        to come for the funeral
        he forbade in his will.

                All too normal that there will never
                        be another
                        evening like this.
                Mom and I drive back
                        in the pink
                        turning violet
                        sunset
                past Friday night teens
                        living it up
                        after-work couples

out for comedy
murder high-adventure and a meal

chattering sprinklers egging
on a thousand lawns
night blooming jasmine
filling the valley
as he is wheeled
out of the elevator.

Washed and wrapped he slides
into the cold room
with the others. No
I decide "it" not "he"
just his husk
drying in the dark
after a long life.
Is there music?
57 years she bedded him.
We pour drinks as usual
sit and talk about him
as if he'd
turned in early
light every candle in the house
go to bed
at eleven
as usual.
Both sleep well.
We were not prepared
to feel so fine.

After   life.

If he'd believed in it
he'd have wanted to return
as penicillin.
During next dawn's run
in the woods where he'd popped
a thousand Nitros and trudged uphill
I consider reincarnation's grace
greet each deer
lizard
brace of quail
fern
and flowering thistle as my father
pass the grove where he'd told me
of the carefully hoaded medicines
he'd given to a friend
who'd used them all
in a painless death
leaving him bereft.
"Can't get any more.
I'll drive to the mountains
lie down in the snow.
Freezing is fast
doesn't hurt as long
as nobody
tries to thaw you out."
I said I wouldn't.

At any rate
pastrami did it faster.
Arnold the wild boar
razor tusked and cork-screw erect
blazes through the manzanita
mounting sows and scattering
joggers
to the March from Aida
which has replaced the wind

while Arnold the Husk
in his silent refrigerator
waits for the harvest
fire.

I run back to my mother
to arrange the cremation.

After two days
Mr. Byrnes
answers his beeper
He'd been in "the field"
of stunned grievers
harvesting cash from ash.
Busy Mr. Byrnes
of "Peninsula Cremation"
with his meat wagon
and his blue jean suit
will transport
cremate
and do the paperwork for $469.00
scatter at sea for $98 extra
plus tax.
"Mr. Byrnes
please....it's been two days
and the family's flying in."
Tuesday is the soonest
he can meet us at the morgue
there's nothing to be done
he's "stacked up"
there are "others ahead."
In the background
the clink of ice
a woman's laugh.

He sounds naked
in a motel room
with whiskey glass
cigarette
urns on the mantel.
"Goddam" he thinks
licking bourbon from her navel
"You want speed
don't die
on a Friday."

No bargaining.
No alternative except to
raid the morgue
reduce him with a chain
saw boil
down the bones ourselves on the stove
hang the pelvis on the mantel
make a drum from the skull
or leave it on the beach
for the pelicans
to balloon in the sun
explode in a stench
that gags the seals.
He would have liked that.
Sea snails in the ventricles
a cormorant's beak between his toes.

His laboratory always stank
of miracles
organic breakdown
the composting fizz
of a maggot's enzyme
the rendering back to the rotten funk
from which something
living
once jumped.

Flo
her womb
many years removed
is still
the magnet.
Sister Sue
her son Jess
arc over the continental flood.
Nothing has ever made the family more immediate.

At the airport I lock
eyes with my sister
dive back off a Saturday morning couch
giggling whispering to let him sleep
later than ever.
We'd spoken in the winter
about such a meeting
staggered our expeditions
so one of us
would be there for Mom
if his knack for scheduling
failed him.

The hierarchy.
Mom supervises
cries when she wants to
vetoes anything
she feels like
finds no argument
finally
gets her way.
Sue the Elder
is rabbinical
phones in the obits
derives a ceremony.
I field
phone calls
make travel
arrangements
confront my middle
age
sneak cigarettes wonder
if I will live so
long so well as he
if I will cry later
if grief is
but a mirror?
Jess waits for assignments.
This is his first death
production.

It's been
three days
drying in the dark
like an old hot-dog
in the back of the fridge
next to the herring
he so loved.
Late nights I'd sneak in with a girl
find him asleep on his feet
in t-shirt and socks
with glass of milk
piece of fish on a fork
before the humming Maytag.
"Good evening" he'd say
and saunter off
the crack of his skinny ass
winking.

We meet with Byrnes.
No muss no fuss no burial
at sea just the basic burn
Byrnes.
He miscalculates the bill in our favor
and takes our check.
How soon?
He'll "do his best."
Mom and I keep poker faced
until he leaves
laugh....
We've cheated death
by sixty dollars.

Not so fast.
Byrnes laughs last later
on the phone
can't cremate
before the ceremony
unless we pay
an extra hundred for a "rush job."
A lot of cases ahead of us.
We're not unique.
We'll pay.
But when can we claim our pot?
Can't wait for delivery
we'll pick it
him
them
it
up. Where? An address
in Oakland.
I try to call ahead.
No such listing.

Finally light.
The doors open.
The rack perfectly designed
by American Morgue Supplies slides out
tilts the body onto the stretcher.
Byrnes rolls through the belly of the hospital humming Merle
Haggard.
Dad gets his minute in the blazing sun
then into the van for the ride to Carbon.

From the gluing of Grandpa's dart
to Grandma's egg
in the dark in the Bronx
His Body.
Cock head
dandelion bobbing in the soap
me between his knees in the bath
His Body!
Fat ring around the navel
sunburned and rosy
captured in a picture
HIS BODY.
As the furnace door
opens
a levee cracks
pigs drown
love makes
a thousand births break water

as a wartime handball partner
survives the same operation
the chest hair I'd twine between my fingers
in the tub
still grows.

HIS BODY!
HIS BODY!
HIS BODY!
HIS BODY!

Perhaps I'll drive to the end of a pier
where coals burn white
in fifty-five gallon drums.
Five dollars for a shovelful of cinders
you bring the bucket.
Byrnes buys in bulk
has a warehouse of boat people
pouring the dust of road-killed dogs
expired winos
ruined chipboard
lawn clippings and chicken bones
into black plastic urns
and pasting on the names.

A Toast. A Smoke
Stack.
Ashes in a filter.
As a biochemical phenomena
he was resolutely teeming wet
dripped buckets at ping-pong
with a rag around his brow
to soak his living up
awed his boy
with horse streams of pee
but now it's finally so divinely 2000 degrees
hot
no sweat.

Not even the mummy
of a virus
could stand this pure
a white.
The fire luck
kept him from
in the Holocaust
but not his Russian cousins
does him right
now.
No Wet.
All Light.
No Body.

California's burnt
brown in the late summer.
I drive over the Bay Bridge
through a haze that's partly his
to the Oakland ghetto
find the gate
a bell and Byrnes apologizing
for the warmth of the urn.
Truly a "rush job."
He pockets the check.
I am not civil
drive off with urn on the front seat
stop on the corner
buckle it in
am stopped by a cop for speeding
no ticket but eyebrows
raised and a warning
"For Gawds sake son take it easy."

42

Mom Sue and Jess wait by the
          carport.
"Who knows what dog they
          mixed
     with Dad?" I say
  invite them to feel
          the hot
          pot.

                    "Holy shit" Jess says.
                  We laugh. It almost is.
          Not shit   not dust   not ashes
                more like the cinders they'd spread
                on the driveway behind the house
                 on Maple Street in the lot
                  where I'd burn the trash
                 in the ashcan light the upside
                   down paper bag's top
                     watch the flame
                    climb the inside
                    and blister out.

My wife calls. She's coming tomorrow.
  Her mother's marooned in St. Jo.
The Missouri keeps rising around her.
          Luckily living
            on the bluffs
              so far
        she's only lost her water.

The brothers are coming
friends and unpopular local relatives.
Neighbors bring macaroni.
We clean.
I take Dad's place
vacuum.

Next morning we're out by seven to the park.
It's a ticketable crime to scatter ashes
on this land.
We pose as a hiking party
water bottle apples and ashes in our lunch pack
stop by the pen of Dad's namesake
Arnold the Boar.
Out of respect for my mother
I don't crack the joke
but she smiles at the pig
and says "there's Arnold"
and my sister's eyes are suddenly hilarious.

Dad's knoll sticks out of the canyon
with a view south
over smoggy San Jose's millions
and up the West Bay Hills
to Candlestick.
There are walkers there in the stubble of oats
which some summer soon
will burn and come back thicker.
"The hay will have its day," I think
and watch the fog lift off the Bay
until the strangers leave and Mom says
"Let's get it over with."

44

I open the urn with my breath
in my chest
and offer the wife first handful.
And the daughter takes a handful
and the grandson
and I.
It's furnace bottom coarse
full of lime
like
concrete.

Mom dusts him out a little at a time.
Sue scatters bird feed.
Jess goes off alone.
I run jump and fling him.
My handfuls
tornado
caught by the updraft
spin off the hill.
Deoxy

Ribo

Silica

Helixes

handful
after handful
glinting in the sun
depart in a flock
towards the Pacific.

45

"Mom! Sue! Look!"
They save some
but let me throw the rest
into the blue.

What a stroke
to watch him disappear so
dry eyed and proud
as if we'd been there
when a comet came close
or a building had blown up
right next to us
to see his bone-chips whirling off
on such a lucky wind
and have the proof that when it rained
when we ate an apple
when we took a lungfull
we'd take him in.

"That's how it's supposed to be"
Mom says
and "Boy I'm glad that's over."
As we walk back the ashes
sting my hands.
I taste him.
Later Sue tells me
that she too
licked her fingers.

On the way back we search for a fitting site
for the ceremony.
An ascent to Dad's knoll
a mile uphill in the sun
would do many of the mourners in
but a cirque of Bay
a tree of thirteen trunks
close to parking
suits Flo's fancy.
Not wanting to unbolt
state property she balks
at my plan to move the picnic tables
into the shade.
"The sun will cook the guests"
I say. She says
"Don't move them"
as if she misses
an argument.

It's been almost a week.

"Whatever Mom wants"
says Sue.
At five I'd learned
that a fist in the stomach
would change her tune
but now I pout
until they cave in.

That afternoon the uncles drop from the sky
    Al
          Sandy
                Marty
                      Bernard.

Uncle Al
with his bad heart
had part raised me.
At the airport
he's bent over but still skis
and all that night that Mom and I
had slept so soundly
Aunt Evelyn had cried and he'd had to hold her.
Al wants to stay with us
to be next door
again
tells me how Pop saved his life once
found him asleep in the snow
on the way in
to Loon Lake
and thawed him out.

Yodeling Sandy
with his bad heart
one day on a hike
at the Depression's peak
had introduced
sweet sixteen sister Flo
to his not quite close friend
Arnold.

Fifty-seven years later Arnold is done
hiking
and Sandy's angina squeezes
him on the uphill
has him and Aunt Bert worried.
They fly in rent a car
come right over.

Kid Brother Marty
smoking still with his bad heart
calls
pissed off as usual.
He and Aunt Mac can't find their son at the airport.
"Where the hell's the little bastard?"
They'll cab into the city.
find him stay with him strangle him
Be there tomorrow
goddammit.

Sonofabitch Bernard
the oldest
with the only good heart
calls to say he's holed up at his son's
won't come over
until the morning.

I want them all to be there
the brothers in the house
grinding his paste
chopping beets for borscht
seasoning his passage
through their bowels
with onions
sour cream
green tomato peppers
slivovitz   vodka   schnapps
Tschaikovksy
tears and howls bawling into the night
the songs of lost Brooklyn.

I pick Dana up at the airport.
Her dad had died three months before
we'd met. "Everything changes after that" she'd said
then changed men
and married me.

Up before dawn
I run to the park
to the Knoll.
My fingers
roll the oats
find not a trace.
Soluble
with the dew
he'd seeped
to the roots.
I run back
to a bustling house.

The Aunties serve a flood
of guests.
Mom swirls
from friend to friend.
Sue and Jess dress
the altar.
I change
greet
handle the phone
keep an eye on the time
keep track of who takes tea
and who's taking too long
so that we'll all go together to Dad's tree
before the sun gets high.
Sandy drives the lead car
Al Dana and I
will bring up the rear.
The house clears.
All depart as planned.
I lock the house
but they've left us
no car.

Nothing like thumbing with your Dad
from a trail-head to the car
on a god-forsaken upstate two lane at night.
Pirates of the road we always got a ride.
He'd taught me this and his brother Al
but now on the busy arterial Boulevard
we have no luck.
Our frantic smiles scare
the cool Californians.

Even Dana
dressed to kill
for the funeral
is passed by.
At last the late Van Robertson
with his dog and daughter-in-law
recognizes Al
pulls over and gives us a lift.

At Van's house
I stood on the roof of a root
cellar in 1953
and watched a hundred miles of Green Mountains
turn blue in the dusk
as they talked about a devil
named McCarthy.
They would go winter camping
Dad and Van Robertson
and on jaunts to Biological Science
conventions in Atlantic City.
After the last one
Dad's stomach went out
and he became an Antiacid man.
He'd burnt a little
hole in his gut
drinking with Van
he confessed
when I went to pee
and found him kneeling
by the stool.

The Bay tree set in photos
fragrantly tells Arnold's time.

Bronx boy grinning monkey
with his Mom.

Muscles and Jewish girls at Coney Island.
Cock-a doodle Daddy.

Hitching with my mother
young on an Adirondack road.

Married in Brooklyn
brick background and bouquet.

Debonair Ph.d
pencil thin moustache.

Pudgy professor with kids and Mrs.
in the sexless fifties.

White haired cosmopolitan
Californian with tan
tales of travels in Hunan

and roses roses roses.

*   *   *   *   *

Sue begins.
We will speak of Dad
in the order of Sandy
Bernard Al Marty and the rest
in the Quaker manner
but first a silent meditation.

I meditate on sitting
on his knee
as he prepared me for nuclear war.
I was five.
"Ten years, fifteen
at most and then a fireball.
We won't feel it
we're so close to the Air
Base it'll be so fast."

I was ready

but after only a moment Bully Bernard breaks
the silence with a strange
interminable speech
he reads from a tiny card
mostly about himself and all the games
he'd taught his little buddy
back in the Bronx.

All I'd heard of Bernard
were of slaps and pinches
that raised bruises
and understand now
why Dad had so hated   chess.

54

I prowl enraged
behind the tables
turn my back on my uncle.
Backhoes are posed
in a field across the way
clawed buckets frozen in the air.
They'd ravaged the flat
pulled out the eucalyptus stumps with chains.
Soon tankers will spray grass
seed in a green mist jellied to stick
and come spring the folks in the pink condos on the hill
will sneeze like hell.
When Bernard is done
I return to the show.

Sandy
visibly pissed
speaks with grace
then Al Marty students colleagues
surprise me recounting
his kindness and generosity
time after time
he'd gone out of his way
for love of them.

I remember that last time he'd whipped us in anger
when Sue had fled the sting
of the clothesline
galloped to the back yard
animal wet-faced mad
roared red through the French doors
and wouldn't come in for hours

He'd shaken in shame through tears
        said he'd never hit again
            and never did.
                Cold
                    distant
                unfaithful to my mother
                arrogant
            intolerant
        withal
    his empathy and affection
                                were memorable.

                Speeches done. The sun
            has the last word, taking the
                ceremony from behind
            sweating collars with its glare.
            "Whew it's hot"
            "Unfortunate circumstances"
            "He was a great guy"
                "Let's eat."
            We return to the house
        drink brag commiserate wonder
                Who's next?
            are congratulated
            for the fine ceremony
            he'd forbidden in his will.
            "He would have liked it".
        My mother has a good time.

Morning.
Dana and I run early
deep into the teeming
hills. Jays racket the woods
flocks of partridge skitter to the
trailside
the deer freeze
wait for us to pass
and as we break out high
in the chapparall above his knoll

                                        a bobcat

    tawny as a bath towel
gives me one yellow eye
    and slinks off.

            I drive to airports.
        Soon the family is down
        again to Mother and me.
    We buy twelve death certificates
    proof to cash in on the pensions
        they'd spent years accruing.
            I avoid talk
        of who gets what.
    Every year he'd sent me new codes
    of Bank Numbers and Funds
        which I'd put unread
        in a file marked FAMILY.
    Nonetheless the next day I depart rich
            in socks.

Last morning.
Too early for Arnold
who sleeps in his pen as I run by
but the deer are up
and the quail and their armies of children
cruise the dew for bugs.
Running the ridge is an easy prelude
to Arnold's mound.
San Jose turns pink to brown
as the rising sun cooks
its exhaust. Cobwebs
on the oats.
No trace.
He's seeped deeper
blown further.

Perhaps a molecule will broach the Rockies
ride the swollen Platte
batter the levee at St Jo
float south to the Gulf
stream east to the Bahamas
north past Hatteras
New Jersey
Cape Cod
Nova Scotia
across to the Hebrides
to be eaten by the herring

he so loved.

To catch a plane
Mom drives me
away.
Once I'm gone she can mourn.
She speaks with relish
of the work it will take to begin life
alone. We kiss
at the metal detector.

No body of land below
this time I fly over Rockies socked in
under glacial vapor
grainy as a slab
halved by a bone saw
marked with occasional plumes and rifts
all the way to the Midwest.
Breaking through sun-glints
on Lake Kansas City
every creek an aneurism
Keokuk sits on the shore of an inland sea.

I descend to the drizzle of home
to the steaming beehive summer city
my wife
my work
in an aching cloud.

And as the fall turns Chicago copper
then white in the snow-most winter remembered
my Mother blossoms.

At Christmas I fly west without a window
or a vision
drive north with Mom to seek the larger family
Aunt Bert and Uncle Sandy
with his bad heart.
We speak little of Dad

though as we drive through the Valley of the Rogue
he's not out of mind
but this is the woman who said
"if I wasn't repressed I'd kill myself"
and he is fifty- five years in her
and he is lost in her.

Later when I ski solo
at Diamond Peak
and sit under a pine
to listen to the silence
he comes back
loud and clear.

Back in January
I write in the dark
seeking the body
lose his details
put the moustache on the child
cannot remember the words to him.
Once I'd asked if he ever imagined what would happen?
"Of course" he said, "and I got it all wrong."

Mom sends the autopsy with the bill.
They really didn't know why
more than his heart was too full
of old arteries
still
they charged Medicaid

forty thousand
        one hundred and fifteen dollars
                        and twenty-two cents

        for that day.

Now I scurry in blue howling freeze-out
past hooded barely thawed figures in the squeaking snow.

No feeling
in my fingers
as I pay phone
Dana to say I'll be late.

When she tells me of her positive test
and that we'll have a kid

red mud again
gushing his body back
know where
my father
know why
the flood

know where my father know why the flood
know where my father know why the flood

know why know why
no why.

March 13, 1994 – Chicago

Of Aurora

Of Aurora

She was conscious
from the ribs
up but cut
off by a screen
couldn't see the gash
from which they pulled
feet first
beslimed with green
her shit-smeared daughter
couldn't feel the cord slicing
that purple squalling part of her away.
I could

see her face
peeled back
belly skin
stomach muscles spread
womb incised
blood full
purple baby grabbed
from a green bag
legs tucked up to show
the swollen lips.
My first thought
"You owe me

"twenty-five dollars."
I'd bet on a girl
She'd bet on
an upside down
jackknifed chin tilted up to look at mother's heart
head too wide from this sky-gazing to pass between the
bones
risking the worst night
mare
a pony stuck half out of her.
Breach.

They'd tried to turn her
three times pushed the bulge
far to the side
but always the head swung back
across the belly like a tide-bound buoy
feet-hooked to pelvis
and looking up
as she does now in swings
at the tilting blue
and coming back and going
branches

the mystery solved when they'd cut in
to get her
seized her
sexed her
sized her
suctioned her pricked her tagged her
wrapped her.
I posed for a picture.
They carried her away.
Her mother just eyes above the oxygen
mask
still half there
died
to hold her.
"When can I hold her?"
"When you can feel
your legs."
The dark spongy pouch
they placed on her ribs
that for one wild moment
I thought was Dana's heart
was the after-birth
big as a bowl.

After   birth.

Calls. Did you cry?
No.
How do you feel? Relieved.
(Is that enough?)
She's fine. Her legs
are coming back.
They're sticking
pins in them now.
She's purple
mad to be out & roaring.

I cigar swagger
down the hall
to the baby aquarium.
Bring on the bill.
I'd won the first roll
of the crap game
the child got
through the mother
the mother got through the knife.
No unmarked stone.
She'll live
long enough
to be named

this
second from the right
marsupial troll.
I count her toes
calibrate the angles
of her ankles
calculate the cost
of any anomaly
read the tag again
to see if she's indeed
the right Baby Girl
my seven pound
six ounce and twenty-one inches
long sperm
result.

So suddenly out.

Dying
to hold her
mother gets her nerves
back
has to
hold her
needs her
ripped up stomach stitched up
tight enough to lift the child
to hard stretched
bulging to burst
breasts.
Bring me that baby.
Empty this
me.

Sex. Poo poo. Sweat. Pee pee.
Tears. Blood. Milk.
Wet business
this life.
In the post-partum
hospital room
hum
woman attached to nipples
too taut
for the butting blind thing to
latch on to.
Smacking squalling dark scarlet & getting hotter
she takes my pinkie with
a mouth so strong
she could hang from the ceiling
by her suck. My nose runs
my eyes water
I'm drowning.
Her epic thirst
will be my drought.
She's got me
by the finger
sleeps
cheeks working.

If she'd died
I'd be free.
What a thought
sits with us
in the dark.
I could sidestep this job
this marriage
duck out
on my own
utterly devasted
of course.
You work this through in birth class
putting the lovely newborn out in the snow
of your mind's dumpster.
A similar infanticide entertained Dana;
the window beckoned
in that hospital room
she tells me six months later
as we spoon porridge
into our laughing perfect
spitting
daughter.

I take my finger back.
She stirs, mews, bleats
then shifts and roars.
Try again. She's not catching
on latching on never will
can't bare the milky mother
Darvon juice
after such rich
umbilical stew
will have to be bottle
broken on expensive
French goat formula
nonetheless will smoke at five
eat wrong
and drink like her
never-satisfied-
Spock-raised
Bottle-sucking
Dadfish.

There are many fronts
to the breast wars.
The woman whom the TV
told that bottles were bad
for baby kept trying and trying
for five days until baby dried up
and died
versus
our mother's titties perfect at sixty
(it wasn't the fashion to nurse
in the fifties)
versus
the stick babies on the news from Rwanda
nursing on the wind.
I feed her. Bottle. She eats. We finally sleep

are woken
an hour later
at six
for latex
eggs
and lactation coach
with pump
and pep talk.
She shows us how
to work the finger in the gum
and slip the nipple in.
Yes
she latches on
finds the trigger
in her mouth,
to eat and now
she's on her way
if she's just an average
American girl
for 74 years.

We finally agree.

Aurora

sleeping beauty

for George Sand
Aurore

for Fuentes
Aura

our first
Light
Dawn

Aurora

water
vowels
her birth-right

Aurora

Aurora

Aurora.

Three days for Ceasareans
then home you go.
Dana
triumphant but raw
at the loading dock
her incision barely knitted
holds the sneezing baby.
I say "Look
the sun
your first sun look daughter."
Blinking in her babycap
she seals her eyes against the blinding fireball
burrows into the dark of her mother.
She'll know the moon first
in her second winter
will look up and point. "Mun."
Later I think
she meant "Man."

And getting her into the Goddammed Car Seat in the
Back Seat
of a stupid Two Door
you realize that with your Twisted Knee and jacked-out
sacral discs
this feather could break your back
and you crawl home as she gasps behind you
her twitching
organ muscle
mouth
sucking in the rich filthy air
protozoans, monoxide, dust. Perhaps TB?
For months a pounding heartbeat
surrounded her
and now six cylinders of BMW
are the next
dominant
lullabye.
She's 3 days out
in the air.

Home. Smarter animals
somehow know to keep it
warm
lick the snot out of its
eyes and nose
let it suck.
Now we cradle a hot coal
and this pink thing burns
holes in our hands
as we read books and phone our
mothers
to ask how a woman with handbag
car keys and earings
will come from this.

Sleep's
welcome
speaks new dangers
death on the lash
of each closed lid.
I learn that beauty
means to trigger fear
that drives me to bend
down with my ear
to catch her breath

to catch her eyes

following anything.

In the constellation of birth
the smallest particle has
the most gravity.
Dana rocks through the night
in her chair sorting
her self out.
My mother
flown in to help for two weeks
loops concentric webs
from the stove
to the fridge
to the baby. I
the neutrino of the house
penetrate the different orbits
come and go
forget about them
for minutes at work
brag in the bar.
The closest I get
is when she sleeps on my stomach
wakes to butt
the hair on my chest with her nose
sputters cranks up to scream
until her mother rolls over
to fold her back in.

First walk
two weeks in the world
swaddled in a bag on my chest
fitttingly enough
an expedition to buy beer.
Come rain come snow
I will dip
her in the world.
I imagine an ocean to show her
migrating birds
against a line of mountains
stretched a hundred
miles above a lake
forests rolling to towered cities
but baptize her in a blurry glint
of phone wires
the el train flashing by
dogs pissing on their leashes
skin of dead November leaves
veining the sidewalk.
Her world of many ceilings
is coming into focus
faces larger than the moon
loom behind fingers
fireballs in the lightbulbs
furniture
cats flickering
in doorways

but a month
in which she's learned to smile
later
when we walk a snowy mile
on Milwaukee Ave.
taking in the neon
the marvelous colorful volcanoes
headlights in the puddles
elephantine busses spraying slush
in the sodium streets
her head bobs
big-eyed out of the baby bag
with pleasure
and I feel better
to know she's glad
to be out
with me

in it.

Infarcation

Infarcation

I. Heartbeat in Seven

Drummer plays quietly in 7/4.

```
        1       2       3       4       5       6       7
thmthm  -   thmthm  -   -   -   thmthm  -  thm   -   -
```

```
bomthabompthabombrrrr   bomthabomthabombrrrrrrrrrbomp
        1       2       3       4       5       6       7
```

Awwwwwww...

Drummer stops mid-beat.

II. The Cold Air

The cold air hurt my skin
The air
Hurt
Cold
Where did you go? Where'd you go?
Where did you go when you were...out?

I dunno.
I was out...

Cold
I was...back

Back where?
Back where you go when you go
Under...
When you go black
for a long time.

30 seconds
could have been the rest of my life.
30 seconds?
Could have been the rest of my life
like THAT!

Drummer in 5/4

1	2	3	4	5
pthm pthm -	pthm pthm	-	pthm pthm	-	-

And I was glad to be back.
Back here?
Back with us?
No. No.
Back with them...the first people.
The first people?
You mean the ones who brought you...

                              High above me....

Back?

Angels
With flippers
And little white uniforms

I saw them.
It was like the old days
When the earth was wild
When the whole earth was wild and the first people sang
I heard their song
When I was coming back.

(starting slow pure high Gregorian with overtones)

Beep Beep Beep Beep Beep Beep Beep Beep Beep....

I'm Back!   On muh back
Looking up at the big eyes
Of the Med Techs.

"Hey...keep your eyes open,
you're doing fine."
(*Whispered*) Ohhhhhhhh...that was close.
"You're doing fine."
That was clossssssssssssssssse.

III. Heartbeat in Five (coming back)

Drums in the dark In 5/4

Some of our mothers thought of us
though they never knew the sum of us or the din of us.
Under the covers the others were done with us
and the dung of us is anonymous isn't it?
Dunning us of all that was coming to us
stunning us with honey
stuh...stuh...stuh...stunting us and hunting us.
All that our lovers had done for which one of us
would be left bereft with the brunt of becoming?
None of us.

IV. So then the Doctor...

So then the doctor comes in and tells you and the missus
what the story is, and how you almost bought the farm
and how lucky you were and how they went up there
and did this and that and they left a little something up in
there, which might or might work, twenty-five percent of
them don't after a while, but most of them do, and again
how lucky you were, and you shouldn't be worrying about
insurance, you should lying flat on your back for two days,
and the pain is from the rib they broke when they were
saving your life and not from the heart, there are no nerves
in the heart, but if you do feel chest pains don't waste a
minute, just ring the bell and take some of these and those
and do this and that, but not *that*, you won't be doing any
of *that* anymore, so don't worry, and above all relax and
then he leaves and so the doctor comes in...

...and tells you and the missus what the story is, and
how you almost bought the farm and how lucky you
were and how they went up there and did this and that
and they left a little something up in there, which might
or might work, twenty-five percent of them don't after
a while, but most of them do, and again how lucky you
were, and you shouldn't be worrying about insurance,
you should lying flat on your back for two days, and the
pain is from the rib they broke when they were saving
your life and not from the heart, there are no nerves
in the heart, but if you do feel chest pains don't waste
a minute, just ring the bell and take some of these and
those and do this and that, but not *that*, you won't be
doing any of *that* anymore, so don't worry, and above all
relax and then he leaves and so the doctor comes in...

V. I will not die standing up

"I will not die standing up."
That's what Bob said when the hammer hit him.
So, will this be the last....
SIT DOWN, they'll see you,

SIT DOWN, they'll see you
keel over.
Will I keel over?
Keel over, keel over, will David keel over?

GET DRESSED!
It's taking too long to
GET DRESSED!

It's taking too long to...
ASK FOR HELP.

You cannot drive.
I could try.
You cannot drive.
I could try.

ASK FOR HELP.

STAND UP.
You can't
STAND UP.
This will pass.
STAND UP.
Ask for help.

This will pass.

Oh my Gawd.
It's not that bad
you're just scared.

YOU'RE GOING TO DIE.
Shut up!
It's just a muscle, not, just a muscle, not,
just a muscle, not...
YOU'RE GOING TO DIE
Shut up!
...that bad.
Oh my Gawd.
YOU'RE GOING TO DIE.
SHUT UP!!!!!

Don't kid yourself.
Stand up.
Get your coat.
Now, walk.
Got your wallet?
Keep walking...
...to the desk.

Hi Fred, Hi Roy.
     ASK FOR HELP.
         Tsup?
             They don't know. He can't tell.

Oh Gawd!
Here it comes, the big one.

Mister, please...

          It's not something I ate...

               that killed my father.

VI. Not Now

No, not now,
just when I'm
falling in love
again, just
when I'm just
learning how.
Not now, just
when I've got
some things
under my belt,
when I'm finally
making sense
and starting to
make my way,
when the
things I've
done are
adding up,
when I'm
becoming
known, when
I'm finally
beginning to
get some
  reward...

Not now,
I'm too
young,
later, when
I'm old,
when I'm
ready, when
I've done
the things I
set out to
do, when
I've built the
foundation,
when I've
made the
harvest,
when the
children
have grown,
when I've
made the
trip to
China,
when I've
made
enough
love, when
I've set the
body of the
dream in
stone...

Not now,
I'm not
ready now,
I'm not
going now,
I'm not. This
cannot be
IT, this
cannot be
the final
bell, last
round, lights
out, closing
whistle,
early curtain
down. No,
not the end,
not like this,
not now, the
end of my
time, not
now, not
here, this
cannot be
the last
thing I will
see, this
hospital
room, that
man...no, not
now...

VII. I'm Back (Reprise)

I'm Back.
From fucking...where?
From where I came back from.
From...
       where I don't remember.
Back from...
I was out...
and I was so happy.

You're doing fine.   That was close.
You're doing fine.   That was close.

VIII. Inside My Heart

Insighhhhhhhhhhhhhhhide my heart is a camera.
In the heart of my heart of my heart of my heart at the end of
a catheter
is a camera.

shoooooooooo   ting   sonar
                        like a blind eye on a stick.
It nosed its way
uptheaortaandaroundthebendanddownintothe
left descending anterior coronary artery

        bouncing SOW WOUNDS
          off the walls of the avalanching avalanche

        bouncing WAY YAYVES
          off the sides of the underwater volcano

bursting in the writhing tunnel
tunnel in the tunnel in the tunnel

                    tunnel.

"INFLATE!" said the surgeon in the purple turban
and the white worm of the balloon butted its way
down the left anterior intercontinental arterial bloodway
                as I watched it
                        on a screen.

If there are no nerves in the heart how can it hurt if there
are no nerves in the heart how can it hurt if there are no
nerves in the heart?

It didn't hurt.
I felt a scraping
      more like a tickling
            no, a scratching
as the turbaned surgeon
snaked the piece of metal into its place.

"DEFLATE!" said the surgeon in the purple turban

and the larval balloon
      condom on a straw
           slipped through the metal ring.

Where the rain never rains and the sun never shines
it's dark as a dungeon way down in the...

        left
             anterior
                   descending
                       arterial
                           coronary
                                 mine.

I saw the sound of it
I saw the sound of it
watched it   pump   squish around
on the screen
like a fish.

IX. I'm Not Going To Try To Be Fine
(Heartbeat in 7 *in 7/4 with drummer*)

I'm not going to try to be fine.
I'm not trying to go over any line.
I'm not living for anyone.
I'm not dying for a reason.

I wanted the world to forget me.
I taunted a sperm to beget me.
The weight of my years contracts me.
The waste of my prayers attacks me.

I'm not going to try to be fine.
I'm not trying to go over any line.
I'm not living for anyone.
I'm not dying for a reason.

X. Smoke Fat

You Smoke Fat Saturated Baby Wimp Whiner Face
breakfast sausage man with that telltale hand on yer
chest and yer eye on yer watch, watch your numbers!
How can you dissolve those mural thrombi
that are gumming you up now even as we speak? Oh yeah!
They're stacked round a core of necrotic material
topped with a fibrous cap. That means,
sclerotic lipids have laminated tight
to yer all too hospitable subintimal regions.
Even worse, the success of percutaneous transmyocardial
revascularization is dependent on you
finding a certified practitioner of the latest modalities
and, oh lord, they're so hard to find!

Infarctic occlusions such as yours
indicate severe stenosis, and that ain't the half of it:
Thrombic instability and lumen compromise
indicate the possibility of severe reocclusion,
formation of lesions, anginal impaction,
necrotic secretions, the end of illusions.

We indicate a cardiac pathology
which we'll now address in layman's terminology.

XI. And So The Guy Next To Me

And so the guy next to me says, he's about sixty and
lean as a fucking greyhound and he's running real fast
without even breaking a sweat, while me I'm huffing and
puffing on the treadmill like an out-of-shape hamster
on the wheel, and I'm thinking, this guy, he's got ten years
on me and look at him go.

And so we're having a conversation about what
brought us both to rehab, and he tells me a story about
the lesion in his ventricle, like a wart on his heart he says,
he's losing his memory and getting tired all the time, so he
goes for a check up and they find this thing, like a potato
he says, like a potato blocking his heart, and then he asks
me and so I tell him about keeling over at the Y and so
he says, "Did they take it out?

And I'm thinking. Take it out? What? He can't be talking
about…but he is, of course, my Ha ha ha ha heart.
That's what they do these days; they take it out to work
on it, they take it out so they can have more room, like with
a motor job, they take it out, they work on it, they clean out
all the old rusty shit, put in new parts, they oil and wax
it, lube it up, then hook up all the tubes and valves and
shit, put it back in and close you up. Mine was out, he
says, not missing a beat on the fucking treadmill, for
57 minutes he says, like it's some sort of record and he's
just full of wonder that it was out and now it's back and
pumping away while he does six miles an hour on the
treadmill and I'm only doing 4.5.

And as he's speaking I can't help but thinking these crazy thoughts, like when they take the heart out, where do they put it? They've got to put it somewhere. There's got to be a special dish the surgeons have for the hearts they take out. And I then I start to visualize it, the heart dish I'll make a fortune with.

It has porcelain loops for all the straps and clamps you need to hold the heart steady so it doesn't pump itself off the dish, onto the floor, out the door and down the hall; it has contoured slots at different levels to secure the various vessels and aortas that come in and out of you, and fluted drains for all the blood. The outside, now this is real high end, a collectors item; it's got beautiful butterfly calligraphy on the lid and on the sides, wow, hand-painted pictures of scenes from heart history, starting with the Greeks, you know, Herotodus, the first diagrams, and then, of course, scenes from the Aztec sacrifices, a priest ripping the heart out of some poor stooge and tossing it down the steps of the pyramid, and then, you know, pictures of the first bypass, a golden stent, and then the first transplant, the face of Dr. Christian Barnard. And who would make them? The Chinese, of course, what, with the normalization of trade, they make porcelain, they got painters up the butt. You could get set up in a factory on the outskirts of Shanghai, hire forty artisans to hand craft these suckers, probably cost you $800 per, go for the real high end market, sell them for 4K to every heart surgeon and cardiac department in the world, with a 30% discount to the patient whose very heart was in the dish, you know, like they could take it home and use it for fondue.

I was gonna ask the potato guy on the treadmill where'd
they stash his ticker for 57 minutes but the buzzer went
off and we had to get off the machines and have blood
pressure taken and then they made us listen to a lecture
on avoiding stress, which went on so long it got me really
pissed off, and then he left and I didn't get a chance to
ask him.

I'm doing the R & D now, working with an artist friend of
mine, but if any of you know, you know, what they put
hearts in when they take them out, let me know, I'll
cut you in, Ha Ha, don't worry, my word is my bond,
cross my heart, Ha Ha. I'm thinking of calling it the
Heart Plate. Get it? Like hot plate? Heart Plate? Once I
get it up, you know, the heart plate, me and my buddy,
we're going to go public, get out an IPO, it's so exciting
you know, like if I don't keel over just working on the
Heart Plate, you know, I'll make a killing.

XII. Tomorrow I'll go Home

Tomorrow I'll go home and live…thirty

                       no, twenty

              no, forty

                  more years

if I eat right and take my pills

            every day

                  for the rest of my life

and avoid
bad fats

and don't get hit by a bus just thinking about

                                      slowing down

every day

            for the rest of my life

and good fats and BAD FATS and how you should
 n't n't n't n't n't n't n't
        need nuts
                or get too upset
                        about cheese.
If I forget may I still be resuscitated?

There's a lot of information f*or which I'm very thankful*
about AutoZone Displays that show what percentage
of your maximum heart rate you're using, with an alarm
feature that goes off when you reach your target zone
not to mention when your brain-dead, and if you were,
would you want to *have to drink a bottle of FAT* that
occurs naturally in fish such as salmon, halibut and *holy
mackerel* everyday for the rest of your life?

There's a lot of information *for which I'm very thankful*,
about medicines like Zocor and Lipitor, ACE inhibitors
HI Fivers, Beta Blockers Metropolol, Toporol, 2B and 2A
antagonists, keelation therapy and the benefits of Prune
Bread, *for which I'm very thankful*, so don't give any
more of your lip-ids mister, and hey, did you know that
RED WINE is an excellent anti-oxidant? So hey, waiter-
nurse, let's have a glass, or 2 or 3 or 4, how bout another
BOTTLE, every day for the rest of my life and while
you're at it, ***MORE BUTTER!***

You lucky bastard, what are you complaining about,
just because you've
   got to got to got to got to
   START NOW,
     making changes like

avoiding STRESS
 management
  every day for the rest of your life
   and taking the time because you've
    got to got to got to got to

take the time to exercise
  every day for the rest of your life.
   Yes, you've got to
    make love vigorously
     every day for the rest of your life.

SLOW BABY SLOW BABY SLOW BABY SLOW
 Down
  and Eat Slow.
   But Don't Eat!
    for the rest of your life.

Just live! Quit your job! Give up your stuff! Go naked in
the street. Dance in the snow.

Remember, you could be
  You almost were
   Maybe you ARE

Dead.

YES, and this is where you went, your <u>life</u> is where you went
when you died. That's when you really lived,
that's when you really danced,
when you keeled over.
That's when you drank red wine.

Right! And you were out for a long time, lucky bastard,
50 years,

you poor shit,
That's not half as long as a sea turtle
        but it's a whole lot longer than a tiger.

So don't forget to take your medi

                        sin

                                phor

                                        physics.

Hey waiter-nurse. I forgot to take my meta-sin-phor
                                twice a day,
                                for the rest of my life,
                                along with my daily
                        cloud –gazing
        fucking

music

and none of it matters because

THERE'S THAT BUS

> and that bus
> and that bus
> and that bus

Drummer plays 7/4

There's always a bus
> to forget about
> > hitting you.

What about somebody else?

Who?
> I don't know.
> > Anyone else.
> > > The surgeon? Right, then where'd you be?

Anything remembered will stop that bus.

> The way the light hit the water
> His remarkable nose
> The melody of crows
> The screeching of trains
> The way she used her hands
> The smell of corn
> The day she was born
> The man sobbing in a window you saw from the El

on this day,
      this day,
         this day,
            this day,
               this day,
                  this day,
                     this day,
                        this day,
                           this day...

in 7/4 with drummer

All of those adored who have gone before
are summoning us, humming to us.
On the rim of falling of the face of us,
the let's be done with this, come with us
to the quietus of us.
The stuh...stuh...stuh...uttering of the base of us,
The stifling of the ba-ba- boom of us,
The muffling of the ...

1	2	3	4	5	6	7
thmthm	- thmthm	-	-	- thmthm	- thm	- -

bomthabompthabombrrrr   bomthabomthabombrrrrrrrrbomp

1	2	3	4	5	6	7

FINIS

108

Fomite

A fomite is a medium capable of transmitting infectious organisms from one individual to another.

"The activity of art is based on the capacity of people to be infected by the feelings of others." Tolstoy, *What Is Art?*

Writing a review on Amazon, Good Reads, Shelfari, Library Thing or other social media sites for readers will help the progress of independent publishing. To submit a review, go to the book page on any of the sites and follow the links for reviews. Books from independent presses rely on reader to reader communications.

Visit http://www.fomitepress.com/FOMITE/Our_Books.html for more information or to order any of our books.

As It Is On Earth
Peter M Wheelwright

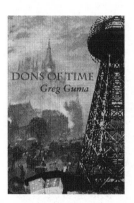

Dons of Time
Greg Guma

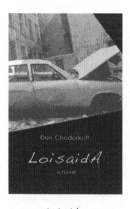

Loisaida
Dan Chodorkoff

My Father's Keeper
Andrew Potok

My God, What Have We Done
Susan V Weiss

Rafi's World
Fred Russell

Fomite

The Co-Conspirator's Tale
Ron Jacobs

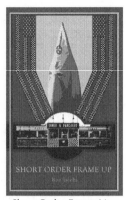
Short Order Frame Up
Ron Jacobs

All the Sinners Saints
Ron Jacobs

Travers' Inferno
L. E. Smith

The Consequence of Gesture
L. E. Smith

Raven or Crow
Joshua Amses

Sinfonia Bulgarica
Zdravka Evtimova

The Good Muslim
of Jackson Heights
Jaysinh Birjépatil

The Moment Before an Injury
Joshua Amses

Fomite

The Return of
Jason Green
Suzi Wizowaty

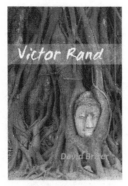

Victor Rand
David Brizeri

Zinsky the Obscure
Ilan Mochari

Body of Work
Andrei Guruianu

Carts and Other Stories
Zdravka Evtimova

Flight
Jay Boyer

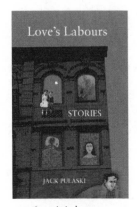

Love's Labours
Jack Pulaski

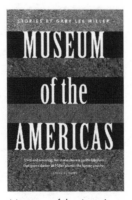

Museum of the Americas
Gary Lee Miller

Saturday Night at Magellan's
Charles Rafferty

Fomite

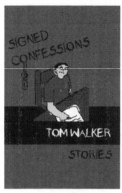

Signed Confessions
Tom Walker

Still Time
Michael Cocchiarale

Suite for Three Voices
Derek Furr

Unfinished Stories of Girls
Catherine Zobal Dent

Views Cost Extra
L. E. Smith

Visiting Hours
Jennifer Anne Moses

When You Remeber
Deir Yassin
R. L. Green

Alfabestiaro
Antonello Borra

Cycling in Plato's Cave
David Cavanagh

Fomite

AlphaBetaBestiario
Antonello Borra

Entanglements
Tony Magistrale

Everyone Lives Here
Sharon Webster

Four-Way Stop
Sherry Olson

Improvisational
Arguments
Anna Faktorovitch

Loosestrife
Greg Delanty

Meanwell
Janice Miller Potter

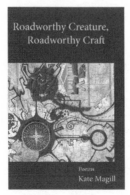

Roadworthy Creature
Roadworth Craft
Kate Magill

The Derivation of
Cowboys & Indians
Joseph D. Reich

Fomite

The Housing Market
Joseph D. Reich

The Empty Notebook
Interrogates Itself
Susan Thomas

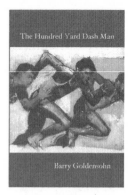

The Hundred Yard
Dash Man
Barry Goldensohn

The Listener Aspires
to the Condition of Music
Barry Goldensohn

The Way None
of This Happened
Mike Breiner

Screwed
Stephen Goldberg

Planet Kasper
Peter Schumann

46369527R00079

Made in the USA
Charleston, SC
12 September 2015